*To Dorothy Aspbury and her
three daughters, Linda, Patty, and Kathy
Love, Gloria*

*For the David-Lang family
–N. C.*

SIMON & SCHUSTER BOOKS FOR YOUNG READERS

An imprint of Simon & Schuster Children's Publishing Division

1230 Avenue of the Americas, New York, New York 10020

Text copyright © 2014 by Gloria Whelan

Illustrations copyright © 2014 by Nancy Carpenter

All rights reserved, including the right of reproduction in whole or in part in any form.

SIMON & SCHUSTER BOOKS FOR YOUNG READERS is a trademark of Simon & Schuster, Inc.

For information about special discounts for bulk purchases, please contact Simon & Schuster Special Sales at 1-866-506-1949 or business@simonandschuster.com.

The Simon & Schuster Speakers Bureau can bring authors to your live event.

For more information or to book an event, contact the Simon & Schuster Speakers Bureau at 1-866-248-3049 or visit our website at www.simonspeakers.com.

Book design by Lucy Ruth Cummins

The text for this book is set in Nicolas Cochin.

The illustrations for this book are rendered digitally.

Manufactured in China

0214 SCP

2 4 6 8 10 9 7 5 3 1

CIP data for this book is available from the Library of Congress.

ISBN 978-1-4169-2753-2

ISBN 978-1-4424-5885-7 (eBook)

Queen Victoria's

BATHING MACHINE

words by GLORIA WHELAN pictures by NANCY CARPENTER

A Paula Wiseman Book

SIMON & SCHUSTER BOOKS FOR YOUNG READERS

NEW YORK LONDON TORONTO SYDNEY NEW DELHI

Queen Victoria looked out at the sea.
It was blue, it was cool, it was nice as could be.
The day was so hot; the sun was so bright.
Her petticoats itched and her corset was tight.
She whispered a wish, it was only a whim.
"How grand it would be to go for a swim."

Her lady-in-waiting collapsed on the floor.
"I've never heard such nonsense before.
Impossible," she cried. "It would be a disgrace
to see more of the queen than her hands and her face.
How would she get from the beach to the water
without showing more of herself than she ought to?"

The queen sighed a sigh. "I'll give up the notion.
I'll never be allowed to enter the ocean.
For how can I swim if I wear all my clothes,
my petticoats and dresses, my shoes and my hose?
They'd get drippy and slushy and soggy and sodden,
and down I would sink right to the bottom."

"My dear," said Prince Albert, "if it is your wish
to dabble and splatter and swim like a fish,
there must be a way to transport you with ease,
while keeping the populace from glimpsing your knees.
I'll give all my genius and all my attention
to devise a device, to invent an invention."

Albert was learned, Albert was bright,
Albert was nearly always right.
He'd been everywhere from Denmark to Munich,
he'd studied old wars both Spartan and Punic.
His knowledge of battles no one could fault.
He'd read dozens of books on the catapult.

It hurled heavy rocks into the air,
chucking them easily from here to there.
"Victoria, dear, it might be romantic
to be launched from your window into the Atlantic.
Moving so quickly you never would show
as much as a peek of your royal toe."

"But, Albert, the English, you know how they shoot
partridge and pheasants, mergansers and coot.
Whatever is up in the air they bring down
and roast it and toast it to a crispy brown,
to have for their breakfast, to have with their tea.
I'm sure you don't wish that to happen to me."

Just after midnight
  Albert sprang from the bed.
A brilliant idea
  had come into his head.
"Wake up, dear Victoria,
  your worries are over.
You can swim all the way
  from Osborne to Dover."

They waltzed, they mazurkaed, they danced a polka or two,
then collapsed on their bed with their nightcaps askew.

First thing in the morning Albert got busy.
His imperial demands made everyone dizzy.
"I must have some wood, quick, cut down a tree.
Dig up some stones and send them to me.
Get me a wheelwright, get me a mason.
Victoria's splashing shan't be confined to a basin."

Albert sawed lumber, he pounded some nails.
He ordered four wheels, he laid down stone rails.
He constructed a room with nary a frown.
He fashioned a porch with steps to climb down.

When all was completed, it was fit for a queen.
"Victoria! I've made you a bathing machine!

"Let me tell you, my dear, what I propose.
You enter the back door wearing all of your clothes.
Off comes your dress, off come your rings,
off come all those unmentionable things.
You put on your suit as quick as can be
and the bathing machine will roll into the sea.

"Once out on the porch the curtain will hide you, while your lady-in-waiting hovers beside you.

"You climb down the steps in perfect repose, into the ocean right up to your nose. No one will get so much as a peep, except for the creatures down in the deep."

"You're a genius, dear Albert, I'm truly excited.
We'll have all the workmen feted and knighted."
She entered the bathing machine by the door.
Off came her corset, ten petticoats, and more.

The windows were shuttered from prying spies,
and her lady-in-waiting covered her eyes.

Good-bye to the land, good-bye to the turf.
Victoria rode the waves and dove into the surf.

Dog paddle, butterfly, sidestroke, and crawl,
the buoyant Victoria attempted them all.
She plunged and she pitched, she rolled and she wallowed,
with water all around her, some of it swallowed.

Two sailors on a frigate were having a tiff,
one said a flatboat, one said a skiff.
"It might be a schooner that has hoisted a sail.
If it gets closer, we'll give it a hail."
"It's taking the shape of a soup tureen.
Belay and avast, I believe it's our queen!"

Victoria, unaware of her subjects' surprise,
carried on with her watery exercise.
Tuna and turtles and salmon and flounder
tickled her toes and swam all around her.
With a splash and a skitter and a final rinse,
the grateful Victoria returned to her prince.

AUTHOR'S NOTE

Victoria became queen of England in 1837 at the age of eighteen. The queen didn't much like Buckingham Palace—too stuffy. She liked Balmoral Castle in Scotland and Osborne House on the Isle of Wight, informal residences where she could relax and enjoy the out-of-doors. She loved to sketch and paint, and was quite good at it. Her children were among her favorite subjects. She also enjoyed pressing flowers from her many ceremonial bouquets.

On February tenth in 1840 Queen Victoria married her cousin Prince Albert of Saxe-Coburg and Gotha, whom she thought very handsome and wise and whom she dearly loved. Together they had nine children and forty-two grandchildren. The children loved to dress up in costumes and put on plays for their parents. It was Prince Albert who designed Osborne House and supervised its building, making sure to follow Victoria's wishes for a residence that was "cheerful and unpalacelike."

The Isle of Wight, Osborne's setting, is in the English Channel and is England's largest island. It has a mild climate and stunning views of the sea from its cliffs. Prince Albert believed that sea bathing was healthy, and encouraged Victoria to swim. The bathing machine was installed at Osborne House in 1846. In her journal Victoria describes driving to the beach with her maids and entering her bathing machine, where she undressed before entering the sea. She wrote on July 30, 1847: "I thought it delightful till I put my head under water, when I thought I should be stifled."

Beginning in 1832 when Victoria was thirteen, she kept a journal, filling 122 volumes with 43,000 pages of descriptions of her children, her husband, court gossip, and the prime ministers with whom she met. The present queen, Elizabeth II, has placed the complete journals online. It's great fun to dip in and out of her life and find what she was thinking. Victoria describes at length her love for her husband, Albert, writing: "He clasped me in his arms, and we kissed each other again and again!"

Despite several frightening assassination attempts, Queen Victoria reigned for sixty-three years, longer than any other British monarch. She died at Osborne House at the age of eighty-one.

After the queen's death, the bathing machine was used for a time as a chicken coop. It has now been restored and may be seen by all who visit Osborne House.

Queen Victoria's bathing machine, Osborne House © English Heritage

Queen Victoria's bathing machine on the Isle of Wight, England, today.

FURTHER READING ABOUT QUEEN VICTORIA THAT YOU MIGHT ENJOY:

Picture Book:

Queen Victoria's Underpants, written by Jackie French and illustrated by Bruce Whatley,
is a charming and funny look under Victoria's voluminous skirts.

For Parents and Teachers:

Becoming Queen Victoria by Kate Williams,
with its stories of her early years, lets you in on all the gossip about
Victoria's dysfunctional family.

Queen Victoria by Lytton Strachey is the most well-known and still the most interesting
biography. Be sure to get the illustrated volume with its delicious pictures.

Queen Victoria's Children by John Van der Kiste
follows the amazing lives of Victoria and Albert's nine children.

Queen Victoria's Sketchbook, with comments by Marina Warner,
is a handsome display of Victoria's sketches and watercolors.

Victoria and Albert: A Family Life at Osborne House by Sarah Ferguson, the
Duchess of York, with Benita Stoney, is an account of a loving couple and caring parents.

Victoria Rebels by Carolyn Meyer
tells the story of Victoria's troubled childhood and her first days
as queen and chronicles her struggle for independence.

We Two: Victoria and Albert: Rulers, Partners, Rivals by Gillian Gill
recounts the ups and downs of this famous marriage.

WEBSITES:

http://www.english-heritage.org.uk/daysout/properties/osborne/beach/queen-victoria/

http://www.bbc.co.uk/history/historic_figures/victoria_queen.shtml

For an opportunity to read Queen Victoria's journals go to
http://www.queenvictoriasjournals.org.